Scholastic Phonics

On a Cruise

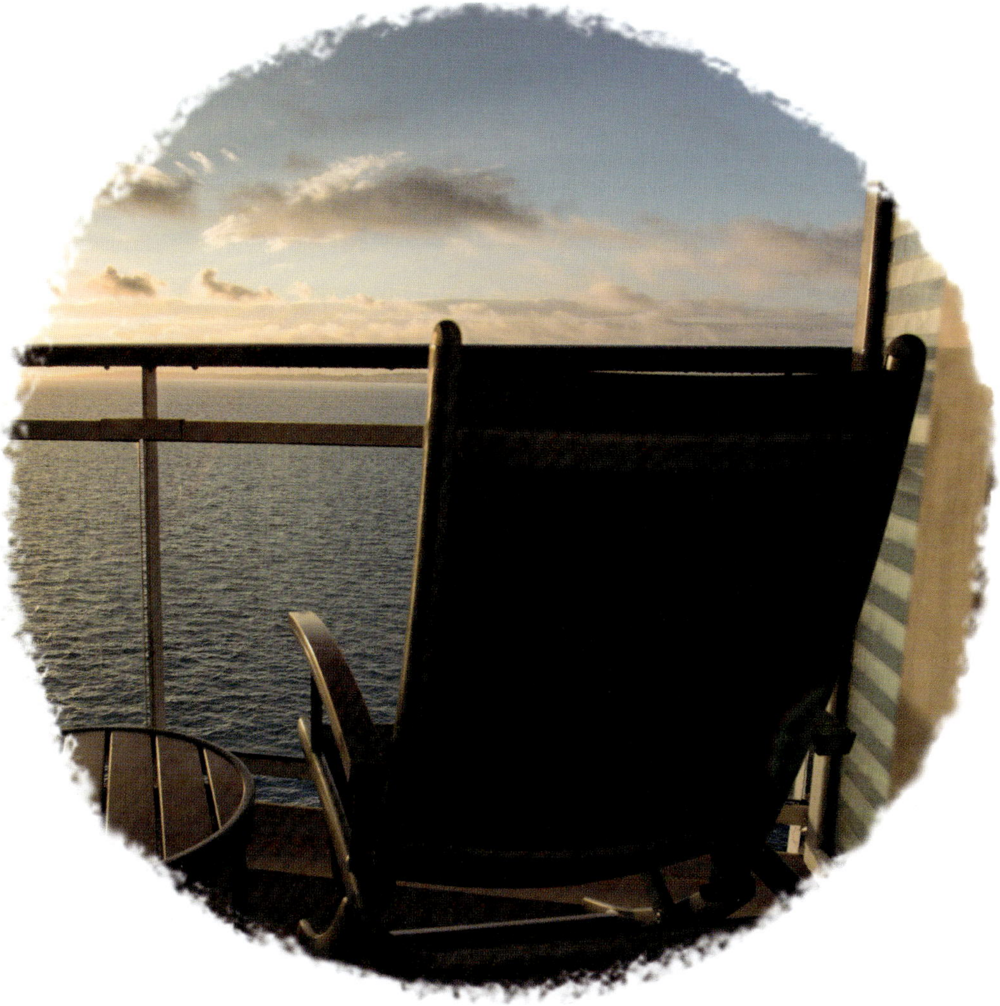

Published in the UK by Scholastic Education, 2023
Scholastic Distribution Centre, Bosworth Avenue, Tournament Fields, Warwick, CV34 6UQ
Scholastic Ireland, 89E Lagan Road, Dublin Industrial Estate, Glasnevin, Dublin, D11 HP5F

SCHOLASTIC and associated logos are trademarks and/or registered trademarks of Scholastic Inc.
www.scholastic.co.uk
© 2023 Scholastic
1 2 3 4 5 6 7 8 9   3 4 5 6 7 8 9 0 1 2

Printed by Ashford Colour Press
The book is made of materials from well-managed, FSC®-certified forests and other controlled sources.

A CIP catalogue record for this book is available from the British Library.
ISBN 978-0702-32112-2

All rights reserved. This book is sold subject to the condition that it shall not, by way of trade or otherwise, be lent, hired out or otherwise circulated in any form of binding or cover other than that in which it is published. No part of this publication may be reproduced, stored in a retrieval system, or transmitted in any form or by any other means (electronic, mechanical, photocopying, recording or otherwise) without prior written permission of Scholastic.

Every effort has been made to trace copyright holders for the works reproduced in this publication, and the publishers apologise for any inadvertent omissions.

Author
Ann Hill

Editorial team
Rachel Morgan, Vicki Yates, Abbie Rushton, Jennie Clifford

Design team
Dipa Mistry, Andrea Lewis, We Are Grace

Illustrations
p8–9 Dan Crisp/Bright Agency

Photographs
Cover jgroup/iStock
p4 Kent Weakley/Shutterstock
p5, 24 Tommy Lee Walker/Shutterstock
p3, 6 Tony Steinberg/Shutterstock
p7 Bryan Busovicki/Shutterstock
p10, 24 ER_09/Shutterstock
p1, 11 grandriver/iStock
p12 eyecrave productions/iStock
p13 Kirk Fisher/Shutterstock
p14 (golf) Irina Wilhauk/Shutterstock
p14 (painting) Dmytro Zinkevych/Shutterstock
p15 (splash pool) Ihor Koptilin/Shutterstock
p15 (indoor pool) Ivan Cholakov/Shutterstock
p16 gbautista87/Shutterstock
p17 BigPixel Photo/Shutterstock
p18, 24 eskystudio/Shutterstock
p19 (city) Halfpoint/Shutterstock
p19 (beach) shutterpix/Shutterstock
p20 Aytug askin/Shutterstock
p21 (chef) LightField Studios/Shutterstock
p21 (waiter) anouchka/iStock
p22 Andreas Vogel/Shutterstock
p23 Pavel L Photo and Video/Shutterstock

Help your child to read!

This book practises these letters and letter sounds.
Point and say the sounds with your child:

- y (as in 'family')
- ea (as in 'breakfast')
- g (as in 'passengers')
- ve (as in 'arrives')
- o (as in 'front')
- se (as in 'cruise')
- ce (as in 'peace')
- ui (as in 'fruit')
- ou (as in 'group')

Your child may need help to read these common tricky words:

- the
- to
- of
- there
- are
- would
- different
- all
- they
- your

Before reading
- Look at the cover picture and read the title together. Read the back cover blurb to your child.
- Ask your child: *What is a cruise ship? Would you like to go on a cruise ship? Why, or why not?*
- Talk about the image in the magnifying glass.

During reading
- If your child gets stuck on a word, remind them to sound it out and then blend the sounds to read the word: p-ea-ce, peace.
- If they are still stuck, show them how to read the word.
- Enjoy looking at the pictures together. Pause to talk about the information.

After reading
- Talk about the images on page 24. What can your child tell you about them?
- Ask your child: *What can you do on a cruise ship? What is the front of a ship called?*
- Discuss what their favourite page in the book was, and why.

Setting off on a cruise is exciting. The ship arrives in the port and waits.

gangway

To get on, you follow the other passengers up the gangway.

When the ship is ready to go, the gangway is raised. The ship sets off. The force of the ship leaves a trail of white froth in the sea.

There is plenty of space for three thousand passengers.

These are the main parts of the cruise ship.

The back is the bow.

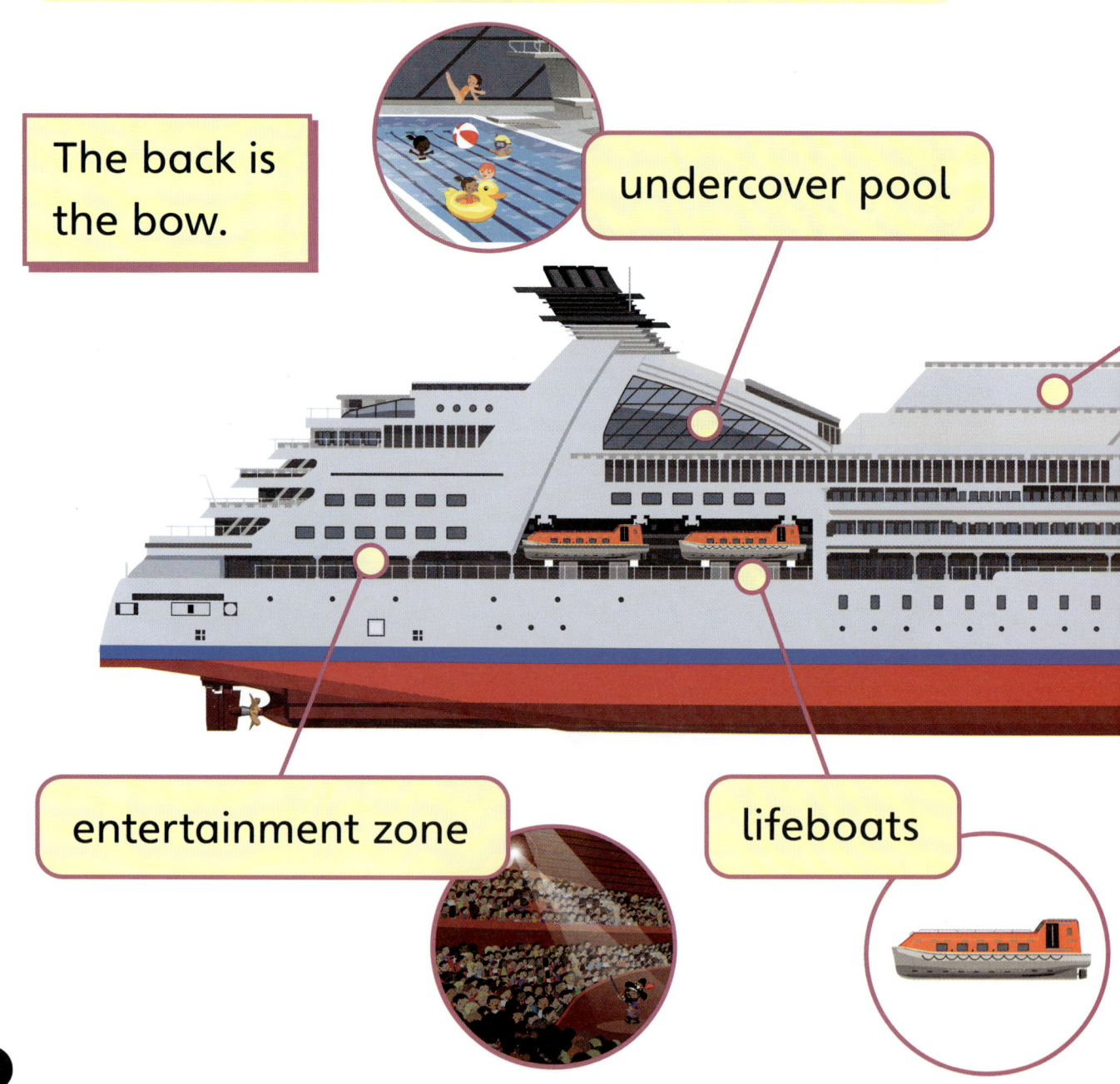

undercover pool

entertainment zone

lifeboats

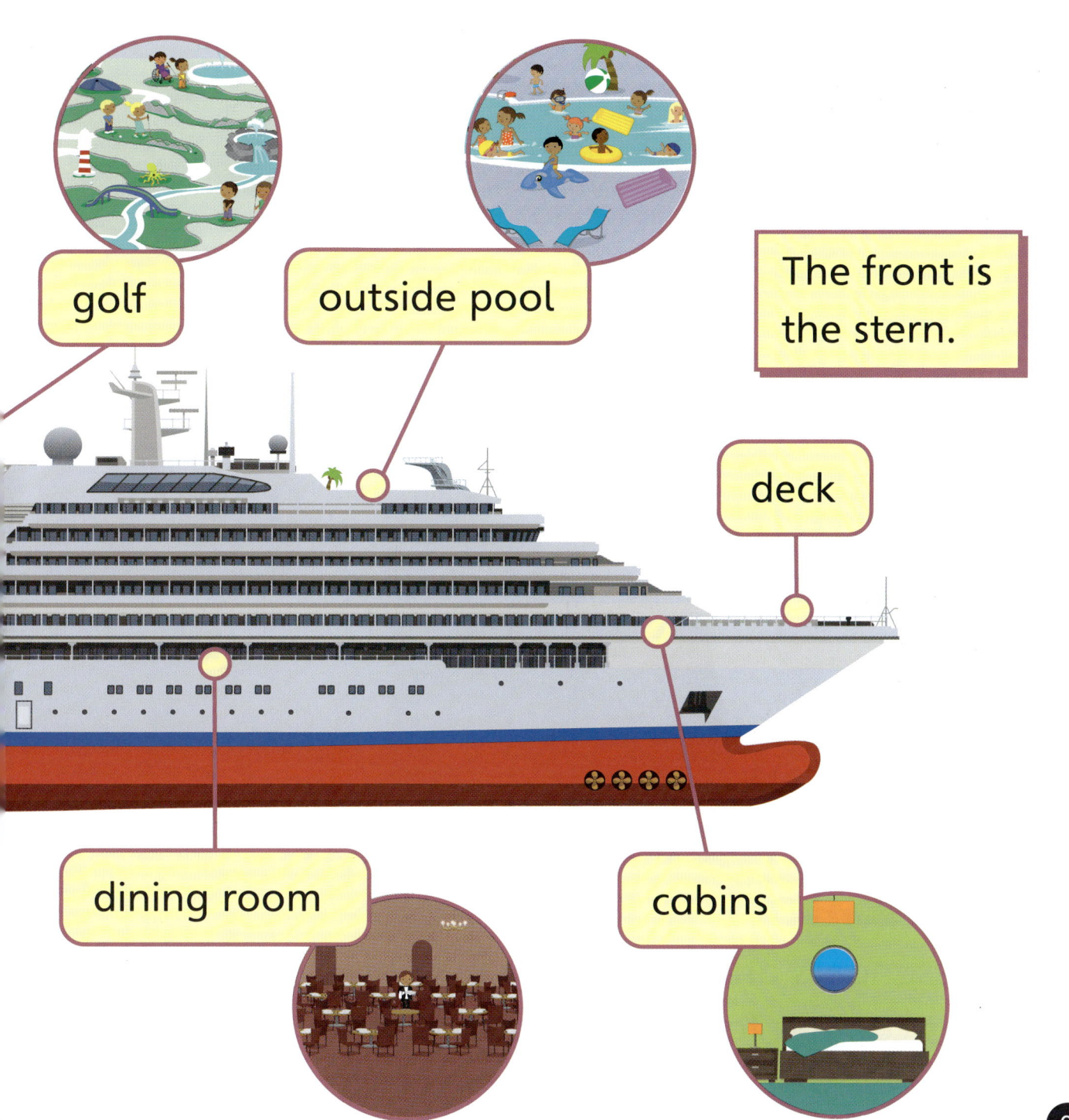

Passengers and crew sleep in cabins. This cabin is for a family group of 4.

balcony

Some cabins have a comfy place to sit and enjoy the peace.

You can have breakfast inside or out on the deck.

You might choose freshly baked bread, buns and fruit. How about a cool juice to drink, too?

There are lots of places to play. Which activity would you choose?

Play golf on the deck.

Draw and paint with groups of other children.

There are outside and undercover swimming pools.

There is lots of entertainment. A stage is set for a play.

There is singing and dancing. Look at her happy face. A cruise is fun!

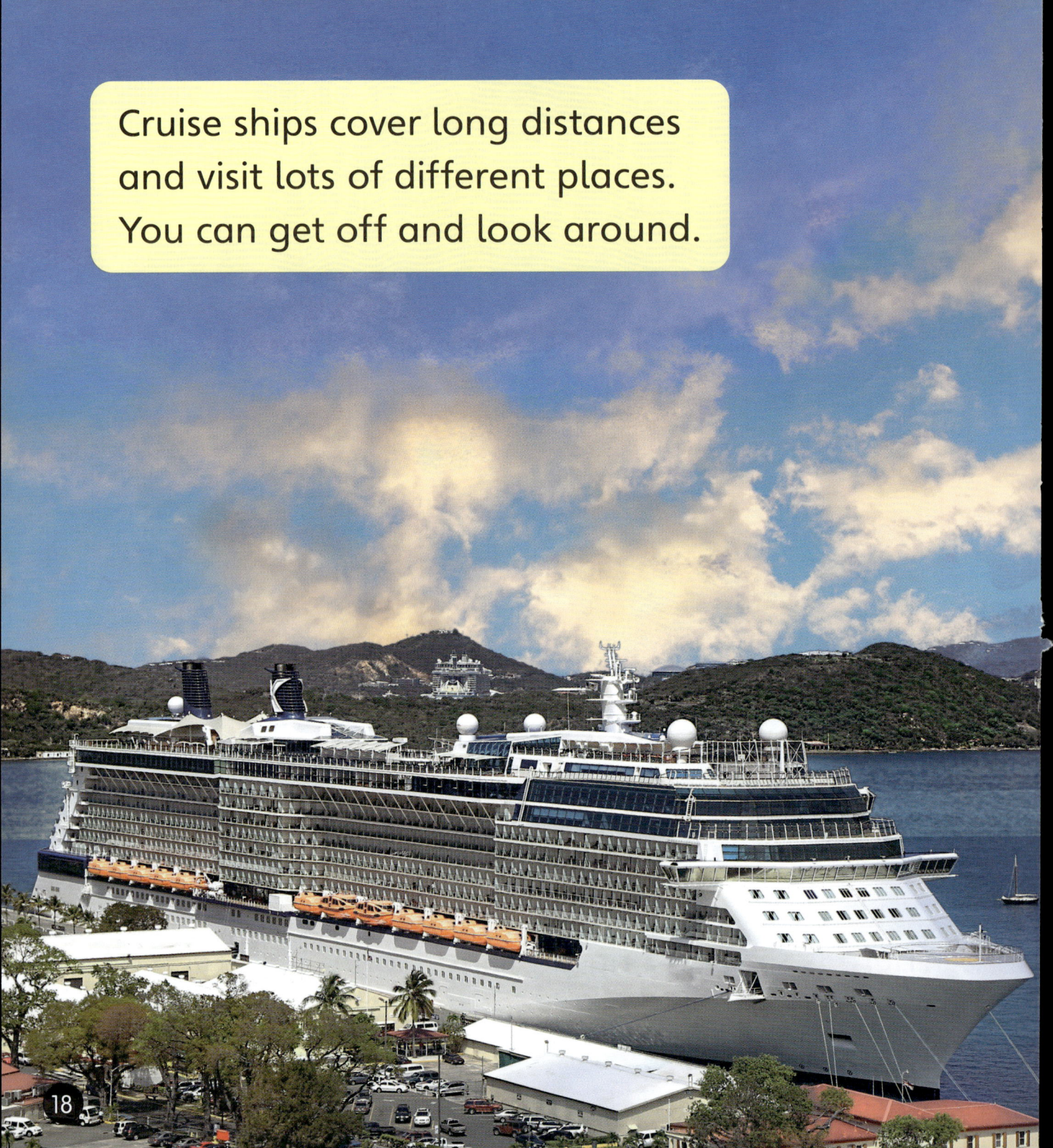

Cruise ships cover long distances and visit lots of different places. You can get off and look around.

This family is sightseeing in a city.

This family is enjoying the beach.

The ship's crew try to keep all the passengers happy. They sail the ship and keep you safe.

Among the crew, you will find cooks, waiters and cleaners.

Sometimes there is a party on the final night. The passengers thank the crew for a lovely time.

In the morning, it is time to pack your suitcase and head home.

Talk about it!